RIM OF THE LOCK

HOUDA K. AL NAAMANI

RIM OF THE LOCK

HOUDA K. AL NAAMANI

DAR HOUDA AL-NAAMANI

RIM OF THE LOCK

Ministry Of Culture and Higher Education
ISBN 978-9953-9009-4-0
Lebanese Agency
Library of Congress cataloging in Publication Data
Nu'mani, Huda ISBN 0-89410-722-4
ISBN 0-89410-723-2

DAR HOUDA AL-NAAMANI
Fouad ST. Dona Maria Beirut Lebanon P.O Box 446

ILLUSTRATIONS

PREFACE

PROF.MIRIAM COOKE
    DUKE UNIVERSITY - U.S.A

KAYSAR AFIF
    POET AND EDITOR
    ALHARAKA ALSHIRYA,
    COLONIA CENTRO-MEXICO

SLEIMAN BAKHTI
    CRITIC AND EDITOR DAR NELSON
    PUBLISHING HOUSE-BEIRUT.LEBANON

My deepest thanks

To Elizabeth Warnock Fernea
Who burned with me in Cairo
the first letters I wrote in English.
A novel still lying in my drawers since 1970.

To Mary Selden Evans
Who has been asking how have I kept my sanity
Despite the horrible events of the war
Believing in Poetry and Love
inspiring those who came across it.

To Miriam Cooke
Who laughed at my remark "Writing is killing me"
By aren't we Don Quixote turning pearls into winds?!
Pearls, when real, fly away
Off themselves
By themselves   For themselves!

To my Dear Lap Top
Beautiful cat with a sapphire eye
vast as the earth
vast as the seven skies
Sign among many of the end of the world.

HESITATIONS

Miriam Cooke

MALLARME ONCE FAMOUSLY DEFINED POETRY AS THE HESITATION BETWEEN SOUND AND MEANING. FIRST, IT IS THE HONEY OF THE HARP AND THEN IT IS A STORY, A LOVE STORY, PERHAPS. FIRST, IT IS THE RUSTLE OF LEAVES AND THEN, PERHAPS, IT IS A THIEF STEALING AWAY THROUGH THE NIGHT. FIRST, IT IS THE MURMUR OF A STREAM AND THEN, PERHAPS, IT IS THE MOTHER CHOKING BACK THE DAILY TEARS. FIRST, IT IS THE "CAMPUS HEDGES SWAM" AND THE "MINT GRAY TEARS" AND THEN IT IS "THE EVIL THING THAT DAY". A COLD, SENSELESS DEATH IN A TIME OF COLD SENSELESS DEATHS

ALTHOUGH HUDA DOES NOT MENTION PRESIDENT KERR'S MURDER, THE TRAGEDY SHE EVOKES TOOK HER BACK WHEN A BRIDE, SHE MARRIED HER COUSIN ABDEL KADER NAAMANI, DEAN OF STUDENTS AFFAIRS AT THAT TIME AND ENTERED THE AMERICAN UNIVERSITY OF CAIRO. HOW FAR WAS THE VIOLENCE TEARING AUB AND BEIRUT APART, FROM THE JOY AND LAUGHTER SHE ENCOUNTERED IN CAIRO. ONLY SIXTEEN YEARS, AMONG THEM THREE SABBATICALS, COULD ANSWER SUCH A QUESTION. HUDA WAS STEEPED IN AMERICAN CULTURE. SHE ATTENDED THE SCHOOL OF ORIENTAL STUDIES, SELECTING ISLAMIC ART AND HISTORY, THEN LITERATURE AND MYSTICISM PURSUING HER SPIRITUAL SEARCH.

FOR THIS POET OF THE UNSEEN, LIFE AND DEATH HAD BECOME ONE, THE SPLENDOR OF THE ONE ENHANCING THE AWE OF THE OTHER. SHE EXHORTS US TO CELEBRATE LIFE WHILE WE STILL HAVE IT. LONG IN THE BARZAKH, IN THAT SPACE BETWEEN HEAVEN AND EARTH THAT IS BOTH HEAVEN AND EARTH AND IS NEITHER, THAT IS THE SWEET OF THE RIVERS AND THE SALT OF THE SEA AND IS NEITHER. OUR LIFE IS PREPARATION. SO LET IT BE MINDFULLY LED, TENDERLY ENGAGED AND LOVINGLY TENDED. EXALT GOD, HUDA WARNS US, AND PREPARE FOR THE HEREAFTER EVEN WHILE NAVIGATING LIFE'S PERILOUS PATHS. "UNLESS PEARLS ARE

POURED" IN THIS TIME OF TRANSIENCE, LIFE WILL BE BETRAYAL, TORMENT AND ILLUSION. IT IS ONLY THE KNOWLEDGE OF GOD'S LOVE AND THE PROMISE OF HEAVEN THAT RENDERS BEARABLE AND ALSO SENSIBLE THE SUFFERING ON EARTH.

HUDA NAAMANI IS THE POET OF PAIN AND VIOLENCE WHO INSISTS ON THE SYMPHONY OF LOVE. THROUGHOUT THE CIVIL WAR IN LEBANON, EVEN IN THOSE MOMENTS OF GREATEST DESPAIR AND SADNESS, SHE WROTE OF LOVE AND THE HUMAN CAPACITY TO TRANSCEND THE EVERYDAY DREAD.

WERE HER PRAYERS ANSWERED IN THE RETURN OF LEBANON, IN THE RISING OF THE PHOENIX OUT OF THE ASHES OF WAR? I BELIEVE THEY WERE. I ALSO BELIEVE THAT WITHOUT HUDA NAAMANI'S POETRY THE WORLD WOULD BE A WORSE PLACE, AN IMPOSSIBLE PLACE.

THIS COLLECTION OF POETRY IS THE FIRST HUDA HAS COMPOSED IN ENGLISH. SHE HAS MADE THIS FOREIGN LANGUAGE HERS IN THE MUSIC OF HER LINES. AND, AS IN THE ARABIC POETRY, SHE HAS MADE NO CONCESSIONS TO HER READER. PLUMBING THE DEPTHS OF THE HUMAN SOUL AND DRAWING ON THE GREAT SUFI MASTERS OF ESOTERIC POETRY, SHE HAS MADE AVAILABLE TO THE NON-ARABIC READER THE INTRICACIES OF THE QUEST FOR THE DIVINE PATH.

WAY WITH WORDS

Kaysar Afif

Whether writing about a mystical experience or describing turmoil, war and violence Huda Naamani has a way with words. She looks, as we all do, at the miserable conditions in this "Broken East" of ours but unlike most of us sees things from a different dimension.

Her position reflects a keen spiritual penetration. To the *"viciously wounded and outrageously injured"* she has one advise : *"Be celestial"* (p. 7)

In lucid simplicity and poetic directness she is asking us to look upwards with complete trust in the Divine to be rescued from our misery.

> Do not doubt   Do not blink
> Do not break   Do not die.

Huda's "Rim of the Lock" reminded me of a Zen story. A Zen Master was asked to restore a broken antique vase kept in the imperial palace for generations. Many artisans before him tried but failed and were executed because many tiny pieces were missing. The Zen master accepted the challenge and started working. In a few days he was done. When the Emperor saw the restored vase he was pleased and awarded the master generously. One of the master's disciples could not but ask the master, " How come the emperor could not see that many pieces were still missing?" "Son", the master answered, "Because the job was done with Love."

It is with this very Love that Huda chooses her words. The magic of this Love is a fire that destroys mediocrity and brings about a mutation. Whatever is said becomes sacred, whatever was seen as broken or fragmented becomes whole again. No matter how ugly

OR OFFENSIVE THE SITUATION MIGHT BE, ITS POETIC EXPRESSION REMAINS BEAUTIFUL.

HUDA'S "RIM OF THE LOCK" IS A CONTINUATION OF HER INNER SEARCHING FOR THE DIVINE. THIS TIME, HOWEVER, SHE SEES HIM IN THE MOST ABSURD AND CONFLICTIVE SITUATIONS, IN THE ATROCITIES OF WARS, CONFESSIONAL STRIFE AND MASSACRES, IN THE BRUTALITY OF MAN TO MAN AND IN THE DULL AND INSENSITIVE EVERYDAY LIFE. THE SUBTLETIES OF THE TEXT ARE ENORMOUS. IF ONE DOES NOT HAVE THE EYES TO SEE BEYOND THE APPARENT HE MIGHT MISS THE FULL RICHNESS. HUDA'S DEPTH OF PERCEPTION DOES NOT COME FROM ABSTRACT THINKING OR FROM "THAT SHARPENED MIND OF OURS" (REPLICA, p39) AS SHE PUTS IT BUT FROM AN INNER VISION. SHE DOES NOT SEEK TO CONDEMN AS A MORALIST OR TO EXPLAIN AS A THEOLOGIAN. RATHER, SHE LOOKS AT THE DIVINE WITH THE TRUSTING EYES OF A SUFI AND SURRENDERS TOTALLY. SHE GOES TO HER INNER SHRINE AND STARTS PRAISING, A TASK SO SIMPLE YET SO DIFFICULT:

> *NOT THAT THE TASK IS MONUMENTAL*
> *I PRAISE   I PRAISE*

SHRINE'S FERVOR P.71

THE "RIM OF THE LOCK" IS ABUNDANT WITH LOVING ENERGY. AS ONE READS IT HE IS LEFT WITH A MYSTERY WHICH IS THAT OF BEING ITSELF. IT IS IN THIS BOOK THAT THE JOURNEY OF A MYSTIC WHO LIVES IN A SOCIETY TORTURED BY MANY ILLS UNFOLDS ITSELF.

FEAST OF SPIRITUALITY

Sleiman Bakhti

In Naamani's poems the reader is openly invited to a feast of spirituality emerging essentially from heartfelt emotions of heightened devotion towards the divine. In truth Naamani's poems are not addressed to the general public but rather seem to drift more to a specific audience who share her tendency towards such matters as faith. The spiritually oriented will find shelter from today's skeptical society in her poems. Those who seek to escape the skepticism, with which this age is now so strongly associated, may resort to Naamani's poems that are rich in topics of both faith and piety.

One may venture to claim that Naamani's poems are her own form of self-defense against a time where reason and science largely overcome both faith and the notion of miracles. Though to our own eyes it may seem that science has triumphed over faith, or reason over miracles, Naamani asserts her position on faith the only way beliefs can be asserted and that is through art and literature thus disregarding or rather opposing the zeitgeist or the spirit of this time.

Her poems reflect her unique style and, in doing so, appear to shed light upon blind faith as a true virtue asserting zestfully "do not doubt!" while stressing that doubt is a sort of sin. These notions and many like them are a throwback to an era where religion had a vast dominance over the masses and its teachings had a large audience.

Such would be the findings of the deepest of reader's yet some poems, Naamani's in particular, seem to hold on the surface sufficient meaning that one need not delve into the realm of implications or symbols. Naamani delights the reader by granting him

THE OPPORTUNITY OF RESTING HIS MIND AND JOURNEYING INTO HER OWN. HER POEMS ENTHRALL THE SHALLOW READER AS WELL AS THE DEEP ONE. BOTH ARE INSTILLED WITH A SENSE OF APPRECIATION OF THE METAPHYSICAL. BOTH EXPERIENCE THE FONDNESS WITH WHICH NAAMANI ADDRESSES SUCH TOPICS AND THE MANNER IN WHICH HER SENTIMENTS FLOW THROUGH THE POEMS ENGULFING THE POEM AND THE READER ALIKE.

HER GOD IS NOT THE HALF-WITTED ONCE RUSSELL MOCKED SO INGENIOUSLY NOR THE FRIGHTENING ONE THE CHURCH USED TO CONTROL THE PEOPLE WITH. HER GOD, THE GOD WE SEE ROAMING DEEP WITHIN HER POEMS, IS THE LOVING AND INSPIRATIONAL FIGURE. HER GOD IS THE PERSONAL GOD. SO PERSONAL IS HE, SO CLOSE, SO INTIMATE, IN FACT, THAT HE MAY NOT EXIST ELSEWHERE OUTSIDE THE POET'S ELABORATE MIND. THIS GOD IS UNIQUE SO THAT, SAY, THE STARVING AFRICAN CHILD MAY NOT FIND HIM OR THE REASONABLE INTELLECTUAL MAY NOT SEE HIM OR THE DEDICATED SCIENTIST MAY NOT DISCOVER HIM. THIS IS THE SIGNIFICANCE OF NAAMANI'S GOD THAT HE LIES SOLELY IN HER POEMS.

GOOD POETS ARE THOSE WHOSE POEMS ARE INSPIRED. GREAT POETS ARE THOSE WHOSE POEMS ARE INSPIRATIONAL. THE DIFFERENCE BETWEEN THE GOOD POET AND THE GREAT ONE IS THE READER. IT IS THE MANNER IN WHICH THE POEM LEAVES YOU THAT ULTIMATELY MAKES THE POEM WORTH READING. THE LESS EFFORT THE READER INVESTS IN UNDERSTANDING A POEM THE WORTHIER IT BECOMES OF THE EFFORT. IT IS THE POEMS' JOB TO UNDERSTAND THE READER AND NOT THE OPPOSITE. NAAMANI'S POEMS DO EXACTLY WHAT IS REQUIRED.

My city is not a city it is a continent.

My home is not a home it is an ocean.

My fire is not a fire it is love.

Jalal Eddin Al Roumi

My Wings are not wings it is infinity.

My dreams are not dreams it is eternity.

Houda K Al - Naamani

INTRODUCTION

Irrelevant is death. Tracing Beirut with sorrow.

raising its flames in verses.

Winds our exclusive secret.

The Ocean, always there breaches infinity

To the farthest dream.

Mountains, blue moon-ships

Wave patched meadows to new endue.

Streams, pillars of fate

Convey wisdom to celestial trumpets

Thirsty as a soul when thirsty.

Lebanon again and again

Enchanted call of longing hands

Poignant hurricane of a broken East.

Lebanon further and further

Bliss of holy shepherds

thrill of constant urge.

Houda

THE BARZAKH*

Since Heaven's knights sought Sublime Path

Had Divine vows failed humanity?

By myriads

Glorious Sun sustains capricious shores

Spacious Stars amend aches of survival

Lavish thunders devote denuded needs.

Let's not hide passions behind rainbow-masks

It is magic though!

Exalted sighs arouse eminent tales

Exuberant sins nourish anguish songs

claimant tears outlast diamonds shells

It is torture though!

Wouldn't flowing to the rim of the lock*

Worth dying for?

TURMOIL OF SCORES

For tribute of alms

When Hazards are alms

Siege Enhances sapphire of myths

Spikes of abbeys.

For tribute of oaths

When lightings are oaths

Omens Engrave slithering of eagles

Folly of mermaids.

For tribute of lust

When night is lust

Visions revere Grails of Prophets

Shields of Prophets

Light attests voices of God   Kingdom of god.

Do not blink   Do not doubt

Do not break   Do not die!

ORACLES IN GRACE

Viciously wounded? Violently injured?

Your lashes dripping blood?

Your eyes dripping blood?

Be Celestial.

Reject vouchers of hells into hells

Discard tokens of omens into omens

Convey puzzle of myths into myths

Rebuke howls of wounds into wounds

Enforce Grace of oracles in oracles.

Whirl Whirl.

Be a beggar

Be a Shepherd

Thousands of white wings

Are whirling with you.

FRAGILITY OF VESSELS

Radiating glare and chills?

Your hands are swirling incense.

Dreading dreams and strife?

Your face your hair are throbbing incense?

Subside bewitched shrouds

heretically tormenting

Deadly besieging

With unbeaten times

Sovereign you are!

Carry the soul of God in your soul

Capture the soul of God in your soul

Ride a magic horse

Strangle Angel of death

Slaying marvels of life

Over our bodies!

STIRRING PURPOSE

Due to forfeit and astray

Due to dust and deceit

May wonders of bliss harshly defying

Be irreversibly presumed

Irrevocably strengthened.

May outrage of trust surprisingly conceived

Be perversely devoted

Drastically engaged.

May demons of space intimately bearing

Be exclusively radiating

Exclusively indulging

Exclusively conveying

A worldwide love

A worldwide belief!

UNLESS PEARLS ARE POURED

Unless

A beaming harbor have been stretched

above a beaming harbor

A bubbling city have been waved

above a bubbling city

An exalting past have been surged

off an exalting past

Splendor is but betrayal

Content is but torment

Recess is but patience

Time is but thorns

Pride is but illusion

ecstasy is but jealousy

Love but massacre.

Denying and affirming

The same quest.

ULTIMATE MIST

Perhaps

For years

We set thresholds   Prodigal thresholds

Spread a thousand honeycombs

beating the rhythm of a timeless bridge

Juggled frail betrothals

scold by tribal pursuits.

Perhaps

For years

We kindled withered gemstones

on spotted pale cheeks

Spared virgin emblems in beaten downtowns.

Never roused a ritual blast!

Never stirred a satanic kiss!

THROUGH MASHRABIA SCREENS*

As if

Greed roamed by

Envy bounced by

Arrogance shook its flints away

Poured raw thyme furrows

On hot wretched borders

Hot wretched idols

Hot wretched envy

Hot wretched decay

Hot wretched conflicts

Hot wretched love.

ABUNDANCE AT DIVERSION

With whelming exuberance

Jasmine and Magnolia trees

induce riddle silken sea

Into voluptuous agonies of romance.

Fig and Almond growth

exalts poised silvery moon

Into ethereal realm of desire.

Statues and altars incite

scented golden hills

Into melodious anthem of earnestness

All of a sudden

Across the glen

From a wide mantle

Dreadful screams flash out ...

PLACE DES CANONS*

Supposing

For a drop of a window   A drop of a staircase

Pledge devotes mirth for commitment

Illusion converts phantasms for appeasing

Sincerity consigns oaths for recovery

Compulsion concedes integrity for reform.

Supposing

For a drop of dispute

A drop of deception

Sacrifice consumes suicide

for a drop of blood

For one little drop of blood...

WOUND HUNT

Therefore

By indigo hues

care enhances identity

Crash back of tedious heritage

need of courteous yield

Gain of spacious reward

Hunger of impatient growth

Portray of forests exertions

Risking another trap

Another rape

Another spell

Another wave of dust.

Initially pink stanzas exhorted

Congenial hearts for a consistent shrine.

ODYSSEY'S ESSENCE

Too much denial to defy

Anguished dams.

Subdued thirst to ravage

Recurrent wells.

Obstinate effigies to strangle

Wailing widows.

Too many knives to slaughter

warfare ravines

Sacked shelters

Shuddered shrines

Fermenting crowds.

Oh!   Prophet kings!

Oh!   Prophet puzzles of our failure!

KNOCK FOR KNOCK

She rather has the field for herself

Tossing a bomb into an ashtray

Terrified by her impotence

Hysterically happy sometimes

Tempted to wipe out an entire source of

Patina.

She often spots a deep cause for getting bored.

Grieves and obsessions

Checked

As

Such.

A.U.B. MELANCHOLY*

As an evil lust that day

Campus hedges swam past reckless waters

Eager briefcases tumbled over magnolia trees.

At both ends

Despaired tapestries trapped deserted corridors

Injured statues turned into bloodless losses

The great gate read no more.

Joyful laughter died out on empty benches

Among diamond earrings

Small drops of rain huddled

Mint gray tears.

SPARKLING AMBUSH

Because

At dawn

Dreams processed abruptly

Melodies gleamed upon domes

Hope leaned towards altars

Gold hands cuddled narrow skirts

Satin belts tossed small breasts.

At length

As a black panther

A black wish was born.

CONSCIOUS ESCAPE

Although yellow ribbons of summer camps

Faded and shivered

Aware and concise

A vivid fragrance of their lives

Was urged to an end...

Tarnished trailers on crawling roads

Rescued distorted shutters

With mourning sighs of remorse.

Organdy dolls glittering like feathers

Led harsh dreams

To another world of realities.

TALISMAN'S GRASP

Should the mountains kneel

Should the mountains pray

Heaven might dissect proofs

Tangible proofs

Whether

Adam and Noah are rolled in one

Abraham and Muhammad are rolled in one

Jesus and the Cross are rolled in one

Life and Death are rolled in one

Earth and skies are rolled in one

You and I

Are rolled in one?

OBVIOUS DEVOTION

How earnestly should pain revere candles

For longing souls

Attend prayer as a lavish princess

Proffer diadems

To enchanted shores

When looted hearts

Conceive queer questions

As how true are trees

Chimneys

And

Lighted windows!

ADORNED INFLICTIONS

Lo! Lo!

The inner blasphemy

Of ancestry in museums

Bearing beside versatile enchantment

The triumphal attire of delight.

Lo! Lo!

The corsair's turmoil of tattooed wrists

The dislodged greed of tinted hair

The profane glamour of bullet-proof jackets

Prescribing for children's graveyards

The breeding ground of terror

The heedless ground of terror.

WITCHCRAFT METAPHOR

Adequately

Wherever bones turn emotional

Waste lands burst in chaos

Myths surge in withered blasts.

Has the emerald jeweler's craft

Gathered all we need

While twisted echoes of lament

Carry nightingale's voice

To mortified ashes?

While Mary's cradle star

Captures the obvious threat to gleam

The olive gaze of prophets

The drop cloth of death?

AS ALL THINGS ARE FORETOLD

Poignant assessments convey

Spiritual appraisals:

Challenge not tormented hearts

Shift not bewildered souls

Capture not monumental fountains

Stress not centennial larks.

Pendent judgments fasten

Entrusted denials:

Agabani turbans will cure obstinate ails

Prayer beads will heal mausoleum lamps

Patriarch rings will assure absentees' return.

In memory of Cana*

More evenings are silent

As shot bodies on astonished hands.

SUBSEQUENT PRIDE

Decidedly embarrassed and discreet

Rides

The red-dyed hair of the fire engine

Twirling playwright in haste

To a wicked trade

Confound era of sharp eccentricity.

Beauty queen

Heading nowhere

In a crimson blaze of

Glory.

JUBILEE

Surely beyond sacrilege

In tousled almond eyes

Divested churches mosques and synagogues

Hasten enchanted spells on holy scrolls

Splash relics of flower-maid pumpkins

On Halloween and Ashoura's masks.

Surely beyond blasphemy

In banished cellars bars

benevolence expels satanic dogmas

On profane blindfolded herds.

haggard mirrors serve looseness

with precarious drinks.

Jubilee of right and wrong

Icons of bladed unwary distortion!

MOSAIC LINKS

Impulse should have conceived better

Anger hasn't leaked yet

"We aspire to innocent provisions

Gigantic roof sheltering us all"

A husky voice stumbled cautiously

Confessing an attempted murder.

"The aim is not parade

But miraculous premises

Clutching gardens of straw on translucent legs"

A reckless voice pleaded constantly

Uttering divine attributes.

Impulse should have perceived better

The worst hasn't poured yet.

DEBATED SACRIFICE

Helping trespassers to trespass

Distributing bread to distribute

Dispensing remedies to dispense

Infiltrating mail to infiltrate

Sustaining apologies to sustain.

Virtue might turn to ashes

Lips to a malicious furnace

Hands to a maiden furor

Eyes to evil wells

Hair to Medusa's snakes.

Behold O God

fervor of exiled shrines.

FILIAL PRISON

Melting on ashes

Rage thawed burgundy candies

Channel stairs carried catering-pouches

to the eleventh floor

Colored snapshots redeemed blush eye-liners

On mocked broken chairs

Sri Lankan maids condensed stabbed-back smiles

From household to household chores.

Hot water out? Electricity off?

Love is reserved for another son

another daughter Studying abroad

- Coming home ! the telephone said.

Cheer is erased by precarious dreams

When chances of living are nil.

FISHING LINE

Even facing the altar

Irony leads to satirical practices

To look for arms

Under your trousers

Between your breasts

To search for a bomb inside your pillow

Behind your icebox

Till you prove your blood group does not forfeit

With this fraction of the city or that

Your expired pass does not divulge

A stimulated libido

A rebuke of a tormented day.

While tomorrow's frame of mind

Can be a heavenly food.

ILLUSIVE SHADOWS

The froggy jackets started yelling

Stepping out of their patrol cars

The bulky boots hurried into the market place

Chasing witnesses like bulldogs

Trapping joggers by shuffle.

Under a tent a blind man

Draping in haste his cauliflowers raised his head

"Let the sky shine for once" he said

"Stop your men. Spare the innocents"

"Let them die!" The armed man answered

Pointing his gun up to the windows

Down to the marble floor

"Enjoy the massacre   you fool"

He added.

From Alpha to Omega

It darely incarnates the felicity of carnage

Children running

Women crying

Houses crumbling

Dying voices slightly audible whispering

Blood   Blood   Blood...

Few years earlier

"Anis" whisked into my hand a glass of wine

"Bassam" brushed on my shoulder a furtive kiss

"Abed" still living asked me to save him a dance.

The weather was orchid

And we were laughing.

BURST OF THE ABYSS

With the utmost speed we fell

in loose eccentricities

Confronting rise of a crazy dollar

Detaching tears from haggard faces

Clipping devices on indolent smiles

Mastering voids of a violent rampage.

-Eggs out of reach? -Water out of reach?

Yet trump tricks were needed to rebuff

a diamond ring onto a finger.

-Your son getting married?

Bidding dummy on air planes attacks?

-Let's play cards!

Stubbornness assumed string-chores

with an aloof tomorrow

Melodies mobilized a suffocating country

A torn country a strangled country

An erased country.

FIERCE SUBMISSION

Disguise your voice when conversing

Secure long gloves as in formal dinners

Affect grace of a pontifical face

Pretend business trips a counter-plot haste

Joint suicides a counter-weight device

Three hour interviews a counter-traffic recipe

Sleep soundly.

Between friction and friction

Consider your enemy a butterfly!

Confronting death

Who would tackle a butterfly?!

WHEEDLING STIMULUS

Meanwhile

As music exploits willow cups at travesty parties

Drinks sustain brass piers on untamed yachts

Laughter feasts large golden hats

under headlong umbrellas.

A sigh nearly a tear flashes inside pain.

Who says war?

Literally you are deported

Your possessions hidden somewhere

Your life buried somewhere.

Has weariness confused your cohesive trust?

Intensified your sinking faith?

Hasn't God called on you Is still calling on you

Shattering your tears with little stars.

Repent Repent

Keep praying   Keep praying.

SMOOTH ASSESSMENT

Until efficiency recuperates its dwell

skill constrains its mess

Bonds shouldn't be foam

Minds shouldn't be strings

Proofs shouldn't be chains.

Flowers should conceive their pollen

Never fictitious   Never false

My heart should preserve its lust

Never hasty   Never abrupt

My hands should attend your depths

Never wicked   Never perverse.

But you are blind

Cynically blind

Endlessly blind.

TREASURE SEAL

By contrast is the rusted Phoenician chest

Attainable

As the golden nymphs of Mercury?

Maps and medals

grievous bestow of dubious pain

Soft assertion of alien seas?

When things can melt down

Like chamber pots

Majestic buildings

Closing their eyes when dying?

INNER LIFE

To many expressionists

Mountains eat each other

Countries eat each other

Men eat each other

Skies eat each other

Gods eat each other

Partly out of hunger

Partly out of love.

ETHEREAL THOUGHTS

A Mickey Mouse pajamas

Grabbed a flashlight

From a Donald Duck pajamas

- Hey! Bring a ladder! I'll jump in!

- Careful! Careful!

Repeated four Bunnies pajamas.

The arguments Attested how intimate bitterness

May discharge eminent bells on lofty fences

May expel hazard from triple cycle outrage.

- Fast!   Fast!

Repeated the four Bunnies pajamas

Knock down the sink we tied last morning

Shatter the lamp we marveled this spring

Destroy the portrait my father revered

all his life.

Nobility? Never say Nobility Milord!

NURTURING ILLUSION

Obviously even legends lapse away

Errance of frightening ghosts

exodus of freezing drafts

recitals of haunted graves

numinous of deadly beasts.

You may rise now Oracles from insane adversities

Distress of endured lands.

Conscious embryos mean roots

honor means warmth

oaths mean protection.

Aware lips will ripen like raisins

Screw lock knots loss

To lock knots rope

To lock knots love.

REPLICA

It sounded off-beat we were not fighting

Allegory withdrew apprehensive zeal

Deception evolved specious doubts:

How long will Kefraya's* dens

Carry a tarnished Milky Way?

Baalbek* Pillars defy a sharp illicit border?

Ryak's* succulent baskets conceal

Infernal cocaine shafts?

How far shall that sharp mind of ours go numb

Facing tenacious infirmities

Confronting wrecked awareness

Besieging cohesive revival

Of a whole earth

screaming?

CORDIAL TRIUMPH

Likely as jasmine temper precedes tea time

Instinct conceives probable boredom

Hunches release heartbreak cajoleries

- Fifth brigade*in charge?

- Barbir Road*on loose?

- Afloat night in Brumana?*

Similarly a fragile moon creates interludes

Between one and another seal

Of episodes.

CRUDE WITCHCRAFT

Few steps apart

Gallant fighters recall cherished memories

Exchange poignant Atabas*

spurred by Katiochas*verves

"Hide not your nipples' glow

behind a drastic pride

Damn the tulle wrap over your scented breast

When would

The full moon Oh little Blossom tear it off?"

Madrigal Drugs charade the looms

of austere torches.

On ripe owls' faces

Only black faith blackens.

SOPHISTICATED CRUST

Seeking to rub terrifying memories?

Sharpen tenderness in perpetual blame?

Wash intensive injuries in reticent tales?

How will sparrows fly and not perceive

an ambush?

Daffodils grow and not speculate a storm?

Rabbits flock and not pursue a train?

Birds survive and not trail a killer?

Had the Sky built our bodies

To embrace shadows?

To warp out cruises?

To beat up chasms?

To deliver desire?

To enhance destiny?

SCATTERED EXULTATION

Feverish is scream of children

In uterus

As in barricaded streets

Wild burst of frowning tears

Storming herds of wriggled witches

Breathed stones of pathetic temple

Suffocated bounce of hollowed balls.

Fervent is scream of children

In uterus

As in sensual feast of eagle's nest

Sanctified wish of concealed drawer

Ravish knock of stubborn pulse

Sacred castration of liberated nations

Amassed star of a revived Earth.

PROMISED EXULTATION

Eminence grips the furrowed face

- It is not I.

Mother last note of a symphony leaves the room.

The moon shaped smile

The inflamed knee

The bouncing heart attack

The tarnished brass vase

- It is not I.

The fossil boned cigarettes

The laughter trend ceremonies

The twigged humorous songs

- It is not I.

The raccoon flesh city

The disrupt fiscal rituals

The robbed avenged delights

- It is not I.   It is not I.   It is not I.

DIVERGENCE OF RELICS

It turns round and round

Reasons to talk about Peace

From sorcery to racial sins

From fantasy to fairytales

From assault to surrender

From elegies to kidnapping

From migration to martyrdom

From malediction to virtue

From partition to divine mercy.

Comparing an "Aya" of the sacred book

With an "Aya" of the same sacred book!

It turns round and round

Reasons to talk about Peace.

CAPTURE

To suppress soft-spoken words

Obvious inquiry of candid eyes

Virtual fury of ceremonial rites

Loud-hard-fast.

To subdue soft-poignant tears

Compelling signal of dubious sways

Fascinating challenge of morbid aches

Loud-hard-fast.

To caress soft-legitimate vaults

Enchanted path of gentle wings

Authentic torrents of limpid approach

Deep-hard-long.

MANIPULATION

A master Mind* is needed

An Alexander   A Salah Ed Deen

To manipulate rivers with mingled threads

To prevent Cherry blossoms from fighting

Pistachios trees from sliding off borders

Black eyes from mastering arms

Banners from up roaring fight.

A Master Mind is needed

to manipulate oceans with mingled threads

An Ibn Khaldun   A Tarek Bin Ziad

A Song of Songs

Tactfully

Discreetly

Peacefully

Joining our hands ... Imminently

Together

PATHETIC HUNT

In search

For enchanting zeal

Clustered centuries-old villages

Adjacent to tolerant stars

Confronting stifled vital discords

Devoting amendable sides of pain

Along deserted restless trailers

Where peaceful courtship thrives

Amorous souls

Convoking as in fairy tales

Blissful sigh of godly green earth

Where heroes on my face not killers

Are kept alive!

HUMBLE SCHEMES

Virtually

hunger is the crow   Thirst is the whore

Ignorance is the fury.

Consequently

Any hedges in these torn fleshes?

Any despair among these drastic blasts?

Should we stand here shivering?

Too long virgin?

Too long chaste?

Nodding was April!   Kneeling was May!

Too long maiden

Too long latent

Mildness implores a latest breed

Ripe peaches dive down from ceilings

Begging exhausted carts

For a last departure.

POIGNANT CRASH

You said you won't survive

You never Scream.

Yet I watch your other selves filled with fright

With constant needs.

You never scream?

I trace the city's murmur in circular lanes

Ascribing your soaking wounds

Errant throb of bewildered hearts

Heavy rain of endless sight.

Bloody shields of divine sight.

You said you seldom lie

In pursuit   as   In elusion

You never cry?

You will survive!

You never scream!

MEGALITH MEGALOMANIA

Somehow

For striking

Committed   We

Immune exemption of abortion

Ironically   We

Sincere infliction of alimony

Legitimate strain of defeat

Paradoxically   We

Irrefutable lapse of distortion

Furtive travesty of

Reptile crypts

Absurd   Absurd   Absurd

BEAT OF THE DEVIL

Sarcastically

Double toil defunct

Paves obituary veils in growling catacombs.

Welcome to Hades!

Above dark burial stretchers

Victim flags roar indignant threats.

Innate phobias screw upper jaw duels

On dagger dance yells.

Gypsies attires bestow coriander spells

In hobble bubble drinks.

Sequentially

Thousand of youngsters

In Feudal clay jars

In haunted mud attics

Pound for Martyrdom.

SULLEN CONVICTION

Cot in cot

By moonlight   As on a pedestal

Phantoms and Specters embrace

Shafting obedient stars on women's scarves

Pouring aura's grace on woeful songs

Rubing bleeding names out of plundered tombs.

War is at rest?

From beyond death   I long for you

With yearning eyes.

- Preys we are?

From beyond life   you grieve for me

With devout eyes.

- Gods we are!

You seem returned   Eternally returned.

SOLEMN COMPULSION

CRUSHED BY OVERWHELMING DESTINY

CENSURED BY CRIMSON GUILT

MINOR INCIDENTS REVEAL HOW GRADUALLY

DAZZLING WATCHMAKERS INSTALL IN WALLS

INTRICATE WHEELS

HOW FREEZING NIGHTMARES SHOWER CHASTENESS

WITH MERCILESS ORGIES

WHEN

RESTLESS APPLE TREES BESTOW ETHEREAL LEAVES

OVER ALL SYMBOLS

BACK TO THE FIRST DAY

OF CREATION!

AS A HAWK* AMONG THE CLOUDS

For them he was a political figure

Just another political figure

For me he was a man who needed help.

I knew I could stretch out my hand

And he would fall like a flower.

When Beirut was burning

Hearing my voice

He burst in forfeit tears.

He is dead now.

But I still hear him

Crying.

FERTILE INITIATION

Afar

We hailed a flamboyant Star

Feasting with a green hooked feather

On a brown flannel hat

sumptuous thoughts

Over grievous abstruse tomorrows.

Close by

We praised a sober seducing Star

Defying by a hell of fringed wafting scarves

His perplexed controversies over

delusive pretence tomorrows.

In dreams

We challenge a disputed tyranny

Invective of a defined extraction

Grasped by two stubborn Giants

Strangling our tight existence.

TALISMAN'S GUARD

Oh ail! Oh ail!

By which hermit dwell

Might sins indulge

Voluptuous call of puberty?

By which soaring pain

Might stress provoke

Passionate strings of sanctity?

By which tender touch

Might flames endure

Capricious cult of ecstasy?

Oh ail! Oh ail!

BANQUET FUGUE

Rest Beirut

Flare of carnelian wines

Fantasy of crimson cliffs

Muse of lavish chains

Yeast of frenzied Cities

Sorcery of nebulous shores.

Rest Beirut

Omen of fermented frost

Mist of ruthless presage

Haze of secret springs

Augur of persistent oaths

Fable of perpetual Epics

Phoenix of an unbound World.

DAY IN   DAY OUT

THE ARCHAIC CHAIRS OF THE "HORSE SHOE"*

ATTRACTED US BLINDLY.

UNDER THE ORNATE MOLDS OF PHOENICIAN TILES

LOVE POEMS MELTED US INTO

A BUNDLE OF AFFECTIONATE CATS.

- WHICH ROAD HAVE YOU CHOSEN?

- WHERE ARE YOU STAYING?

WE ASKED NEWCOMERS.

IN PRELUDE

SETTLERS WERE PERVERSELY HURT

IF AMONG THE TINY DISHES OF MEZZA*

THEY WEREN'T SERVED AS SNACKS AND APPETIZERS.

IN COLONIAL BEIRUT

A DALIA'S HEART WAS ALL WE NEEDED.

BLAZING FITNESS

Tempered by her grandfather Siberian furs

Spanish dotted leather gloves.

Aroused by her Grandmother* agate combs

English carved ivory fans.

Stirred by her Aunt beaded satin shoes

French embroidered velvet lace.

Seduced by her Mother*

Scented Turkish baths

Ritual night-play boudoirs.

But

Screwed to her own blue shirt

Diaspora pains stitched with silver yarn

To her ebony skin.

N'EST CE PAS? N'EST CE PAS?

-Mmm fantastic!

Along the raucous lanes of resorts

The tense markets of shining prawns

Straw baskets of fried mussels

Cheers conflicted courtships of regional tastes

Charcoal chops recalled childhood dilemmas.

- Air raids in the South?

- Voiture piegée in Bliss?

Assumption pacified defeated pride.

Hustle fermented limestone Narguilas.

Hammer-steps Debka revoked Valentine Balloons.

Ruby eyes justified jewels crimes.

Most evocative

These agonizing aromas!

CALL IT " DISGRACE WAR "

Since intellects exert stagger brain songs

On margin silk mattresses

Fairness of five Turkish crowns.

Since perverse clerks release fuel

With sacks of flour

Cost of fast intercourse Delight of football fans.

Since snipers personify watch burglars watch rats

Scrabbling Circumcision knives

Under travestied tanks.

Since farcical kisses distribute

false gaiety false appetite

On dancers' bosoms late each night.

Since Foot invaders blow colossal words

in colossal horns:

Do not panic neighbors! Do not return dogs!

78

MAJESTIC STRINGS

For epics

Goat nursed Gods

Cascades of rosary beads

Canvas of waterfalls

Storms of twilights

That emerald Rock* of angelic tints

That Red Rose

Possessed by the Holy Ghost

With a thrilling touch

Of ecstasy.

SUBLIME RECURRENCE

Vulnerable to the heartbeat of God
Adjacent to doomed galleys Hijack kidnappings
Verdict of belligerent asylums
Pursuit of illicit fate.

Vulnerable to the hand pulse of God
Adjacent to whirling cyclones Edgy sermons
of scaffold's shadows
Perverse madness of vendettas wails.

Vulnerable to the vengeful claws of God
Adjacent to rusted hooves of petrified tanks
Repel of tangled bars on twisted women's necks.

Disguised consciousness
Of green bulbous eyes
Of an enormous Turtle.

INVINCIBLE FIRMAMENT

The more you taste His Thrill in you

Arch of alien stars

Sway of aching flesh

Eagle of magic spell

Garden of prodigal flames

The more He tests His Light in you

Convey of weeping Cross

Diadem of repentant threat

Game of surfeit host

Pledge of awaited truce

Version of ninety-nine names!

THE DITCH*

Trapped in a lost cage

a lost city   a lost continent

Under the assessment of

Hundreds of scholars Hundreds of microscopes

Hundreds of light bulbs.

- Half Arab! Half Muslim! Half Terrorist!

The microscopes say.

Sentence is death.

- Half robot! Half slave! Half animal!

The light bulbs say.

Sentence is death.

- Half sperm! Half killer! Half monster!

The scholars say.

Sentence is death.

Books a felony!   Right Wrong a joke!

The Mouse uttered to himself.

HEALING

You should slowly breathe His presence

Holy journey   Substantial lodge.

Gladly trace His glory

Shining arrows upon your walls.

Gently conceal His promise

Lavish palace upon the sky.

Blindly shed His laughter

Magic Island in both your hands.

But here you are

Erecting sculptures

With heavy clouds like barricades.

SIX HUNDRED THOUSAND WHISKERS*

They said for the door was small

They said for my worship

They said for descent of sins

They said for legitimate subtractions

They said for merit of two faced time

They said for the wedding of "Hamza and Ra"*

They said for the essence of "Perhaps"

They said for disjoining comprehension

They said for concern of short debates

They said for distance of twelve hundred miles

They said for release of the black stone

They said for crashing against a desert

They said for inheriting a temple

They said for watering a target

They said for annulling a parchment

They said for establishing a translucent rank

They said for reaching an eternal life

They said for stopping a flock of birds

They said for a loss

Of six hundred thousand whiskers

They said for the ultimate sign of Gemini

They said for consecutive readings

They said for a triplicate loss

They said for an innate question

They said for a safe return

They said for a single "Aya"*.

Oh! Blessed is grief if it is love

Love if it is death

Death if it is a journey.

You who never abstain

Never depart

You have no home but I.

A MOUTH ENGRAVED IN MARBLE*

Long since the night whispered to the night

As though whispers had roots

Whispers had sharpness

Whispers had a mouth engraved in marble

Whispers had a cradle shaped in heaven

Whispers had a father and a mother

Whispers had a liturgy and moons

Whispers had temples and dômes

Whispers had deities and thrones.

You said light is a veil

Darkness is a veil

Blue hides in Your Eyes

I write blue on Your hands!

I write my hands on Your hands!

It is the soul shining again!

CONFORM EXERTION

Restraining Neptunian distortion?

Centennial relief is merging in!

Attending pontificate drizzle?

Tenacious cure is launching in!

Ascribing pretended elixir?

Nuptial bless is diving in!

Denouncing persistent curse

Die Die Die again

Revised concept is racing in!

Prevailing equity is landing in!

ENTHUSIASM

Ethical and esoteric

The piano quartet we hear.

Dropping beads in ascetic hands

Chilled rhythms in besieged sands

Converged pulse of rational minds.

Tormented and erroneous

The deceptive remedy we perceive

Windmills of ambushed wheels

Slaughter of a labeled loss

Plea of a fermented love

Breath of a surviving nation.

APPROPRIATE ALLEGIANCE

Apart of chief foretelling

Shields are apt to widen.

Turn into obstinate hosts.

Expose mortified ashes to

Genuine era of venerated flesh.

A Mahdi fervently

Recounted!

A Messiah ritually

Recalled!

VISITOR MERGER

What ring shall I wear?

What country shall I seek?

Burdens assert drastic duplicities.

Exert claims for an Eternal life.

Jesus is coming.

Continuous pursuit of vigilant Skies

Indefinite Journey of a united world

pledge fear of a conveyed cross.

Jesus is coming.

For thus we kneel

Mystify life as much as Death

Pursue death as much as life.

ASTRAL ENIGMA

Of all His ancestors

Particularly slow He moves

Promised signal of burning light

Released challenge of subtle trust

Here and there He walks in search for omens.

At His feet -He knows-

Nurtured travesties will capitulate.

Sectarian tolls will conceive

Assigned access of relief.

Sturdy assertion will haunt

Consistent vouchers of rebounds.

Forever - He knows-

Proof will annul racial obsession

Of disputes.

CATTLE PASS

If those Stones scarcely human evoke

sacred coffins of Sheltered creeds

Will Solomon's seal exalts glorious epics

With celestial winds?

Will Jesus' journey hasten evangelical rescue

With ultimate plead?

Will Infant's fragrance bestow lucid remedies

With peaceful banners?

Will Kaaba's cloak nurture rhythmic calls

With final zeal?

TO SLIDE SLIDE AGAIN

Granted an underline sign of depth?

Ultimate proportion of compassion?

Impressive panic when lonely selves have

no issues?

Game mirrors of unknown trap?

Expunged for the time being off somewhere?

Sublime ability of distinctive thrones

Where many skies lay on top of others?

Device hills have alternatives

As verve span   as age speed!

Last time I checked myself I was centuries older

Toy notion of strain? Hem echo of errant width?

Smooth masquerade one carries and hide?

squad of fairies sounds,

like curtains! Curtains!

SHRINE'S FERVOR

Not that the task is monumental

I praise   I praise

Fair felicity arises

Stepping off   from our skins.

Those same madmen are ill-fated lovers.

Holiness emanates from rebellious shrines.

Clemency nourishes genuine convictions.

Tolerance derives from revived cults.

Oh ! God

I praise   I praise

RESURRECT CONVICTION

May I say Throne?

May I say Angels?

May I say Sparrows?

Songs of initiated trust

Rescue of prominent heart.

May I say Message?

May I say oath?

May I say peace?

Conscience of awaited essence

Nucleus of infinite Reign?

CAPRICE

Nearly no double chin.

No swelling cheeks

No bewildered heart

No pageant horns.

Nearly no notorious landmarks.

No ruthless names

No criminal features

No prevailing draft

No capricious end.

But entangled destinies

A blue sea

And white lilies!

*THE TRUMPET**

At last

exemption is dispensing persistent death.

Detention is releasing intimate warmth.

Repentance is repealing seduced casts.

Accession is pursuing genuine crowns.

As by oracles

Oh! God

Sheep and wolves are espousing.

Earth and sky are contesting.

Flowers and trees are throbbing.

Cradles and tombs are merging.

By Your adornments God

Is it dawn again?

Glossary

*THE BARZAKH: Predictable Bridge in Islam, where after death spirits meet, sift and purify, awaiting the Day of resurrection.

*RIM OF THE LOCK: Of a Pejorative Door, leading to redemption, through religious tasks and duties. The crossing here is also political. Suggests International understanding by assets of love and forgiveness.

*PEARLS: Symbol of asceticism and purity.

*Mashrabias Screens: Woven Bay of multitude small wood-cuts, allow outlets view to indoors. Used by warriors as battles shields.

*PLACE DES CANONS: Centre Ville of Beirut, demolished at the beginning of the war, establishing a deadly margin between the two sections of the city.

*A.U.B. MELANCHOLY: assassination's Day of President Malcolm Kerr, aggravating tragically the human course of civil war.

*Cana: City in South Lebanon honored in Christian Mythology with its Messianic relics sculpted on its walls. It endured attacks of Israeli Planes in 1999 again 2006, causing drastic casualties among young children.

*Kefraya: Village in Bekaa Valley, known for the best vineyards, best squeezing cells, the best wines. Among them Arak, a Lebanese specialty.

*Baalbek City: Home of the Great Roman Temple where a yearly International Festival is held, mostly at Bacchus amphitheatre, presenting traditional and fresh musicals programs by renown Arabs and famous International Stars.

*Ryak City: Border Town in Bekaa, known for its military airport and commercial relations with Syria.

*Fifth brigade: Multi-religious corps in the Lebanese Army that have stationed on the Green Line during the last phase of the two years War.

*Barbir Road: Foot path between East and West of Beirut. Remained open during the worst courses of military events.

*Brumana: Summer Resort in Christian sector used freely and safely by all confessional groups throughout violence.

98

*Atabas: Romantic musical dialects of old times recited up to now on Rababeh or Oud in summer festivals and family gatherings.

*Katiochas: Weapons introduced first by Palestinian Factions, used afterwards by Lebanese sectors on both sides.

*Master Mind: For perversity of divergences born during the war from National Policies and International interferences.

*Blown as a Hawk : Respect to Sunni Prime Minister Rashid Karame, killed in a helicopter blast in 1989, on his way to his office in Beirut.

*Horse Shoe: Famous Café in Hamra where Poets and Artists used to meet. Moved later to Sadat street. Carries now the name of City Café.

Mezza: Small appetizers known as Lebanese specialties.*

*Abdel Wahab el Ghazzi: Syrian notable whose son Said, became Head of Parliament then Prime Minister during Shukri Kouwatly's regime.

*Salwa Ghazzi: Houda's mother. Early pioneer in Syrian Feminist movement. Married Fouad Naamani and moved to Beirut.

*Pigeon Rock: Lebanese landmark on the Lebanese Shore.

*THE DITCH: An imagined narrative tale of the unfortunate political and cultural misunderstanding between East and West.

*Six hundred thousand whiskers *Mouth engraved in Marble: Poems from "DOT ON H" read at "One o'clock" IMF visitors Center-World Bank Washington – 1990. Registered in Arabic at the Library of Congress.

*"Hamza and Ra" Hint to the debate between classical and modern poetry.

*"Aya" Short Koranic verse.

*THE Trumpet: Signal to the last Day on Earth. Call of ascendance of Human souls to the eternal world.

Table of Contents

BY THE POET

TO YOU	DAR AL NAHAR	1970
MY FINGERS NOT		1971
LOVE POEM	DAR AN NAHAR	1973
1 REMEMBER I WAS A POINT I WAS A CIRCLE		
	DAR AN NAHAR	1978
"H" TUMBLING ON THE SNOW	DAR AN NAHAR	1982
VISION ON A THRONE	AL MOASSASSEH AL ARABIA	1989
HOUDA I AM THE LORD	DAR HOUDA AL. NAAMANI	1991
1 WAS A POINT I WAS A CIRCLE		
	THREE CONTINENTS PRESS	1993
KITAB EL WAJD	DAR HOUDA AL. NAAMANI	1998
POETRY READING CASSETTE		
	DAR HOUDA AL. NAAMANI	1989
LE RAVISSEMENT DU TONNERRE LES AMIS DE LA POÉSIE		1999
TRADUIT DE L'ARABE PAR CLARA MURNER ET ROULA NABULSI		
MANY LIPS, YOU HAVE SHEPHERD MANY HANDS		
	DAR HOUDA AL. NAAMANI	2001
A DOT ON "H"	DAR HOUDA AL. NAAMANI	2004
TO WHOM IS THE EARTH TO WHOM IS GOD		
	DAR HOUDA AL. NAAMANI	2006

One thousand copies
Were printed on Japanese paper   chamois 120 gram.
Printed by Nahhal EST. Beirut - Lebanon
Designed by Ahmad Khaled